Contents

What's Special about Coastal Habitats?

Saltmarshes; fast-drying sand dunes; slacks (flat, low-lying land between dunes, that are ponds in winter and marshes for most of summer); steep rocky shores with tiny soil-filled crevices; craggy cliffs; meadows sloping gently down to sandy beaches or gravelly inlets – the very varied coastline of Wales provides habitats for a great variety of wildflowers.

While some flowers thrive on exposure to sunlight and prevailing wind, others relish shade and shelter from salt spray. Tenacious plants spring from crevices in splintered rocks, while orchids thrive in coastal meadows where granite gives way to nutrient-rich limestone. Not surprisingly, some of our rarest wildflowers are to be found near seashores.

Open Access

Most of the coastline of Wales is easily accessible and, both scenically and in terms of floral diversity, extremely rich. As a result the coast is a much-visited part of our countryside. The UK Day Visits Survey found that in 1998 trips to the coastline of Wales topped the 22 million mark.

In 1970 the Pembrokeshire Coast Path was opened by the famous Welsh writer and broadcaster Wynford Vaughan Thomas. The original route has been slightly extended and now comprises an unbroken 186 miles of footpath from Poppit Sands, near Cardigan, to Amroth in South Pembrokeshire.

Spring and early summer are the best times for wildflowers along the cliff-tops and hedge banks on this spectacular coastal trail.

Fifteen of the 67 National Nature Reserves in Wales are on the coast or sufficiently close to the sea that their floral diversity is very much influenced by the seaside climate. Wildflowers that could not survive the extremes of temperature and drought found further inland thrive in sheltered seaside nooks and crannies and in the unique habitats created by gradually shifting sand dunes or weathering limestone cliffs.

On Anglesey, the reserve at Newborough Warren includes active and stable dunes, saltmarshes and mudflats as well as dune areas planted with pine trees. Morfa Harlech is one of Britain's few accreting sand dune systems, acquiring material via the long-shore drift that is currently eroding the dunes further down the Coast at Morfa Dyffryn. Compared with more stable areas, dynamic habitats of this type have fewer species, but they are often home to some quite rare wildflowers that elsewhere would be crowded out by more vigorous plants.

South Wales also has its share of botanic treasures. For scenic beauty and floral interest the Gower National Nature Reserve, with the Worm's Head and limestone cliffs, is hard to beat. Nearer to Swansea, at Oxwich more than 600 wildflower species have been recorded. Heading east towards Cardiff, the nature reserve at Kenfig Dunes is particularly lovely in summer, when the dunes and cliffs are covered with pyramidal orchids, dune pansies, sea holly and (quite literally) hundreds of other wildflower species.

Finally to an enigma: Crymlyn Bog is an extensive area of lowland fen. It lies in the floodplain of the River Neath, near its estuary, and provides habitat more typical of East Anglia. There are swamps, water meadows, reed beds, waterlogged willow scrub and damp woodland. No wonder, then, that this coastal reserve holds such a diversity of wildlife as well as some rare and very beautiful wildflowers.

5

Spring Squill *(Scilla verna)*

These lovely lilies carpet favoured grassy cliffs of Wales in May and early June. With their short, strong stems they are ideally adapted to such exposed windswept locations. Although usually blue, the flowers are sometimes mauve and occasionally white.

14mm

A member of the family Liliaceae, spring squill is sometimes mistaken for a stunted bluebell. Worldwide there are nearly 100 species in the *Scilla* genus, most of which bloom in springtime.

In Greek mythology Scylla and Charybdis were sea monsters that lived on opposite sides of a narrow channel. Scylla had a woman's face and torso, but from her flanks grew six necks each with the head of a vicious dog; she also had twelve canine legs and a fish's tail.

Sailors attempting to avoid Charybdis would pass too close to Scylla, and *vice versa* – hence the phrase 'between Scylla and Charybdis', meaning trapped between two dangers.

Jan Feb Mar Apr May Jun Jul Aug Sep Oct Nov Dec

Rock Sea-spurry *(Spergularia rupicola)*

Distinguishing the various species of sea-spurry is far from easy, as all have pinkish-violet flowers with five un-notched petals. Rock sea-spurry clings to rocky cliffs and sea walls, notably on the north and west coasts of Wales. **Greater sea-spurry, *Spergularia media*,** is found mainly in the drier edges of saltmarshes, while **lesser sea-spurry (*Spergularia marina*)** has smaller flowers than either rock sea-spurrey or greater sea-spurrey.

< 9mm >

Rock sea-spurrey is one of more than 200 wildflowers that can be seen on the cliffs of Skomer Island.

Sea-spurreys are rarely abundant anywhere in Wales, but the cliffs at Kenfig Nature Reserve and the Pembrokeshire Coast Path are very good places to look for these attractive perennial (although just occasionally annual) members of the family Caryophyllaceae.

Jan   Feb   Mar   Apr   May   Jun   Jul   Aug   Sep   Oct   Nov   Dec

Green-winged Orchid *(Anacamptis morio)*

< 10mm >

Green veins on the three sepals that form the hood of the flowers of this orchid clearly distinguish this species from the various other purple orchids of springtime.

The flowers of the green-winged orchid have a faint, sweet scent. They vary tremendously in colour, from reddish-purple (very similar to the **early purple orchid, *Orchis mascula*)** to pale pink and even white. Most sizeable colonies of green-winged orchids will contain plants of each colour. The upper part of the flower is helmet-like in appearance.

This wild orchid is relatively rare in Wales, but it can be found along the South Wales coast and on the western edge of Snowdonia National Park. Outside Wales, green-winged orchids are found mainly in damp grassland.

Jan   Feb   Mar   Apr   May   Jun   Jul   Aug   Sep   Oct   Nov   Dec   *9*

Sea Campion *(Silene uniflora)*

Beside cliff-top paths, from rock crevices and even in shingle above the high-tide mark, the bobbing heads of sea campion attract butterflies, moths and other insects. It has larger flowers than **bladder campion, *Silene vulgaris*,** with which it is sometimes confused.

< 22mm >

Mainly a wildflower of the coast, sea campion (a member of the family Caryophyllaceae) also grows inland beside some mountain streams. Our pictures were taken on the Pembrokeshire Coast Path, but sea campion occurs in many other coastal locations in Wales including the Great Orme, where the much rarer bloody cranesbill can also be seen.

Marbled coronet moths lay their eggs within the seed pods of sea campion and its relative, bladder campion.

Thrift *(Armeria maritima)*

Commonly known as sea pinks, tufts of thrift are scattered like cushions all along the cliffs and saltmarshes of Wales. This lovely plant, which produces flowers in just about every possible shade of pink, copes well with salt spray and even the occasional inundation.

< 35mm >

The origin of the common name of this plant may refer to the tight formation of the leaves, which helps thrift to conserve its freshwater content in the salty coastal winds. Perhaps significantly, thrift was the plant featured on the back of the brass-nickel threepenny bit (a three-old-pence coin) which was minted up until 1970.

On some of the rocky headlands of Anglesey, the Lleyn Peninsula, Ceredigion and Pembrokeshire these perennial wildflowers grow in such profusion that grass is scarcely visible between the brilliant pink clumps.

Thrift belongs to the family Plumbaginaceae, as also do the various species of sea-lavender (see page 49).

Jan   Feb   Mar   Apr   May   Jun   Jul   Aug   Sep   Oct   Nov   Dec   *11*

Common Scurvygrass *(Cochlearia officinalis)*

>9mm<

A member of the cabbage family, Brassicaceae, common scurvygrass is so called because of its former use to treat scurvy. This disease, caused by vitamin C deficiency, was common among sailors who did not have regular supplies of fruit and vegetables.

Common scurvygrass grows in great abundance on cliffs, on roadside banks, and in ditches and drier edges of saltmarshes throughout Wales, often extending several miles inland. Although usually white, the flowers are occasionally mauve.

In recent years the central reservations of motorways and many other main road verges have been colonised by **Danish scurvygrass – *Cochlearia danica*** - an early-flowering prostrate species with small (4mm across) white or lilac flowers. The salt that is spread on roads to prevent icing in winter seems to have created ideal habitat for this carpeting wildflower, which continues blooming sporadically all through the summer months.

Wild Carrot *(Daucus carota)*

60mm

This familiar plant (a relative of the edible carrot) grows in profusion in virtually all coastal habitats and can be found in some inland locations too, including roadside verges.

Wild carrot, which belongs to the umbellifer family Apiaceae, has several common names including Queen Anne's Lace. There are many stories of the English queen's association with this plant. One of these refers to the small purple floret that is often found in the centre of the flower head. While doing lacework, the queen is said to have pricked her finger, leaving a purple bloodstain in the middle of the lace.

Although a biennial, wild carrot produces many seeds and spreads quickly, so that once established it is extremely difficult to eradicate.

Kidney Vetch *(Anthyllis vulneraria)*

This wildflower favours grassy and rocky habitats on limestone and chalk and is especially common on stable sand dunes and on limestone-based coastal slopes throughout Wales.

< 30mm >

The flower head of this member of the pea family, Fabiaceae, forms a distinct kidney shape. Although usually deep yellow the flowers also occur in orange, red, white and even purple from time to time.

Kidney vetch grows in profusion at Oxwich, on the Gower Peninsula in South Wales. There the population of the small blue butterfly (*Cupido minimus*) has shown signs of increasing – bucking a UK-wide downward trend. These rare butterflies lay their eggs on kidney vetch, where the larvae subsequently develop.

Alexanders *(Smyrnium olusatrum)*

50mm

The large glossy leaves of this member of the carrot family, Apiaceae, distinguish it from other yellow-flowered umbellifers with which it might otherwise be confused.

As the flowers mature so the unpleasant smell of alexanders becomes more intense; then, like most other umbellifers, this tall wildflower becomes a great attractor of insects. It seems to be particularly popular with shield bugs and hoverflies.

Commonly seen on roadsides, cliffs and wasteland near the sea, alexanders is an infrequent sight more than a mile or two away from the sea.

The name 'alexanders' comes from the country of Macedonia, birthplace of Alexander the Great, where this plant is most plentiful.

The Romans brought this plant in to Britain for culinary purposes, and in the past the roots of alexanders were cooked - they are rather like parsnips - and the leaves were used in salads.

Jan   Feb   Mar   Apr   May   Jun   Jul   Aug   Sep   Oct   Nov   Dec   *15*

Early Marsh-orchid *(Dactylorhiza incarnata)*

40mm

These beautiful spring-flowering orchids grow in profusion in the dune slacks at Ynyslas, Morfa Dyffryn and Morfa Harlech; at Newborough Warren on Anglesey; down the West Wales coast to the Gower Peninsula and Oxwich; and at Kenfig National Nature Reserve.

Early marsh-orchids also occur in fens, marshes and bogs and on the shores of some lowland lakes.

Subspecies of this orchid range from purple through bright red and flesh pink to pale yellow.

Jan   Feb   Mar   Apr   May   Jun   Jul   Aug   Sep   Oct   Nov   Dec

The flesh-pink subspecies *Dactylorhiza incarnata* ssp. *incarnata* often grows together with a purple variant, *pulchella,* and the less common bright red *coccinea.*

< 15mm >

To further complicate identification, the various subspecies of early marsh-orchids hybridise with one another as well as with other *Dactyloriza* species including the southern marsh-orchid and the northern marsh-orchid, both of which occur in Wales.

Tufted Vetch *(Vicia cracca)*

By far the most conspicuous of our common vetches, this perennial plant with its showy tufts of flowers clings by means of tendrils to hedges, cliff-tops and grassy banks.

< 25mm >

Found in all kinds of open habitats throughout Wales, nowhere is tufted vetch more showy than when smothering the fence beside a coastal path with its one-sided racemes of indigo-blue flowers.

Tufted vetch is an important source of food for one of our rarest butterflies, the wood white (*Leptidea sinapis*). This butterfly is seen mainly in woodland clearings and under coastal cliffs, and in recent years its numbers have declined significantly.

In common with the many other kinds of vetch found in Wales, tufted vetch is a member of the pea family, Fabaceae.

Sea Bindweed *(Calystegia soldanella)*

This creeping perennial is commonly found growing on dunes and occasionally in shingle on the shores of Wales. Kidney-shaped leaves, and flowers with noticeably yellowish centres, distinguish sea bindweed from the other members of the family Convolvulaceae.

< 45mm >

The bell-like flowers of sea bindweed have five white stripes similar to those of field bindweed. This plant is not a climber, however, as unlike other bindweeds it does not have tendrils.

An attractive and tenacious coloniser of shifting sand dunes, sea bindweed is found in all coastal parts of Wales.

Jan   Feb   Mar   Apr   May   Jun   Jul   Aug   Sep   Oct   Nov   Dec   *19*

Tormentil *(Potentilla erecta)*

Tormentil is an acid-loving plant that thrives on coastal cliffs and gravelly freshwater inlets. You will also find this summer wildflower in Welsh mountain and moorland habitats.

< 9mm >

Tormina is the Latin for colic, for which ailment tormentil was used as a herbal treatment. There are also records of the root of this member of the rose family, Rosaceae, being used to make an astringent powder for treating gum disease. It has also been used to treat the wounds of battle as well as mouth ulcers and even sunburn.

Artists produced a red dye from the roots of tormentil – thus explaining why one of its common names is bloodroot – and in Lapland it is still used today to stain leather. Tormentil is also used to flavour certain kinds of schnapps.

Tree Mallow *(Lavatera arborea)*

< **40mm** >

Growing up to three metres tall, tree mallow is a Mediterranean-Atlantic biennial that thrives in wasteland near the sea and on sheltered coastal cliffs.

Tree mallow is our only woody native member of the family Malvaceae.

Roseate terns sometimes nest against the roots of tree mallow; however, these attractive seaside plants are not good news for all birds. There are concerns that on some rocky islands climate change is favouring tree mallow to the point where it is now smothering nesting areas previously used by puffins.

Jan   Feb   Mar   Apr   May   Jun   Jul   Aug   Sep   Oct   Nov   Dec   *21*

Sea Stock *(Matthiola sinuata)*

One of the rarest of Britain's coastal wildflowers, wild sea stock is a Red Book species. It is native to cliffs and sand dunes, and apart from a tiny area of North Devon it is now mainly confined to the South Wales coastal strip between Cardiff and Swansea.

< 20mm >

The night-scented pale purple flowers and woolly grey leaves of this distinctive short-lived perennial fall to leave a tangle of long, curved seed pods.

Currently at the northern extreme of its range here in Wales, this attractive wildflower may become more widespread if the current climate change trend continues.

Sea stock is a member of the cabbage family, Brassicaceae.

Rock Samphire *(Crithmum maritimum)*

The fleshy leaf spikes of this bright yellow-green umbellifer and its restriction to coastal habitats make rock samphire very easy to identify.

< 50mm >

In the past, this plant was collected from rocky ledges and stable shingle shores to be used in the treatment of kidney disorders. It was also considered to help cure obesity and, enigmatically, to improve the digestion.

A member of the family Apiaceae Rock samphire, also referred to as sea fennel, can be added to salads or pickled in vinegar and spices.

Stinking Iris *(Iris foetidissima)*

An infrequent wildflower found along the South Wales coast and in the Dee and Clwyd Valleys, the pale flowers of stinking iris produce orange seeds that persist into winter.

One of only two truly native irises (the other being the yellow Flag Iris, *Iris pseudacorus*) stinking iris is a lime-loving perennial plant that favours scrub, woodland edges and cliffs near the sea. Its derogatory common name comes not from the scent of the flowers but from the smell of its sap when the leaves are crushed.

The iris family, Iridaceae, was named after the rainbow goddess Iris who, in Greek mythology, was keeper of the rainbow. (Worldwide, the colour range of irises is vast.) As a winged messenger of the Olympic gods, Iris travelled back and forth between heaven and earth.

Irises have also been used since ancient times as medicinal plants; indeed, in the fourth century BC the use of stinking iris was referred to by Theophrastus, favourite pupil of the Greek philosopher Aristotle, when he was attempting to classify plants and to describe their structure, habits and uses.

Sea Mayweed *(Tripleurospermum maritimum)*

One of several similar members of the daisy family, Asteraceae, sea mayweed is a sprawling annual/biennial that grows in shingle, stone walls and other bare seaside places.

35mm

Sea mayweed is a great coloniser of shifting sand above the high-tide mark, and it therefore provides a valuable first-line of defence against erosion.

Several other species of mayweed - some scented, others unscented - can be found in Wales. For example, **pineappleweed, *Matricaria discoidea***, originally from Asia, is now widespread throughout Wales and the rest of the UK. Common on cultivated farmland, this plant also occurs frequently on roadsides. When crushed the flowers smell distinctly of pineapple.

Gorse *(Ulex europaeus)*

A fine spring day on the Gower Peninsula: the unmistakable sweet coconut scent of gorse wafting on the breeze is one of the essential pleasures of walking the coastal footpaths of Wales. Somewhere along the way you will find gorse in bloom during every month of the year, but at no time is this prickly bush more gloriously golden than in the month of May.

Gorse provides wonderful habitat for small birds, whose nests therein are virtually impregnable to raiding predators. Insects, such as the hawthorn fly seen here, are also attracted to the scented flowers.

In the past gorse, a member of the pea family, Fabiaceae, was used as an under thatch on Welsh cottages before laying down the final layer of straw.

Grass of Parnassus *(Parnassia palustris)*

Not a grass at all but a member of the saxifrage family, Saxifragaceae, grass of Parnassus is limited in its distribution in Wales to the northern coastal strip and Anglesey. The dune slacks of Newborough Warren provide stunning displays of this lovely flower of marsh, fen and damp grassland.

The name of this wildflower is a reference to Mount Parnassus, in Greece, where it is reputed that at one time this plant carpeted the whole of the mountainside like grass.

Jan   Feb   Mar   Apr   May   Jun   Jul   Aug   Sep   Oct   Nov   Dec   *27*

Dune Pansy *(Viola tricolor* ssp. *curtisii)*

Inland, most wild pansies (*Viola tricolor*) are blue or blue-and-yellow and they are either annuals or biennials; the lower-growing maritime subspecies *curtisii* is a perennial and, although sometimes entirely or mainly blue, its flowers are more often yellow.

< 20mm >

Commonly called dune pansies, these pretty little flowers all face in the same direction – towards the sunny south – on the flanks of stable sand dunes such as those along the North Wales coast, at Pembrey Burrows and at Kenfig.

Pansies are members of the family Violaceae.

Lady's Bedstraw *(Galium verum)*

With its scent similar to new-mown hay this common coastal plant was once used to fill mattresses. It was also reputedly used in cheese making: when boiled, a strong solution distilled from the plant curdled milk and coloured the resulting cheese yellow.

> 3 <
mm

The coastal cliffs of Wales, particularly in chalk and limestone areas, and the dry slopes of stable sand dunes are the favoured habitats of lady's bedstraw, although this plant does sometimes occur in dry wayside habitats, meadows and heathland.

Of the numerous members of the bedstraw family, Rubiaceae, lady's bedstraw is the easiest to identify: it is the only one with yellow flowers. In the past it was used to dye wool yellow.

Jan   Feb   Mar   Apr   May   Jun   Jul   Aug   Sep   Oct   Nov   Dec   *29*

Round-leaved Wintergreen *(Pyrola rotundifolia)*

Jan   Feb   Mar   Apr   May   Jun   Jul   Aug   Sep   Oct   Nov   Dec

Persisting all through the winter, the neat round leaves of this nationally scarce wildflower of calcareous dune slacks are a great aid to locating plant colonies.

Throughout most of coastal Wales, round-leaved wintergreen is scarce and quite difficult to find. The flowers appear at the same time as, and in the kinds of places favoured by, many other small white flowers that bloom in much greater abundance. For example, in some of the dunes slacks of Kenfig National Nature Reserve the dense carpets of marsh helleborines often conceal small pockets of round-leaved wintergreen, usually on the drier edges of the slacks.

The best display we have ever seen of these lovely summer flowers was at Newborough Warren, on Anglesey, one of Wales's finest National Nature Reserves for wildflowers.

The white, downward tilted flowers of round-leaved wintergreen are distinguished by a central ring of ten bright orange stamens. When fully out they are more open than the flowers of other species in the wintergreen family, Pyrolaceae.

In sheltered spots, desiccated flowers of round-leaved wintergreen sometimes persist well into the winter months.

Haresfoot Clover *(Trifolium arvense)*

A sand-dune flower generally more common on acid soils than in chalk or limestone regions, haresfoot clover also occurs inland in dry, sandy grassland. The flower heads are usually pink but occasionally white.

This pretty plant grows in profusion close to the seashore at Kenfig Dunes and at Newborough Warren, where it favours the edges of well-worn paths. Its common name refers to the shape and the soft and downy feel of the flower heads.

Each tiny flower of this member of the pea family, Fabiaceae, is shrouded by pale brown sepals, so that even when freshly opened haresfoot clover has rather a 'dried hay' appearance.

< 20mm >

English Stonecrop *(Sedum anglicum)*

The rocky shores of Wales provide ideal habitat for this beautiful succulent wildflower.

< 12mm >

Like other members of the stonecrop family, Crassulaceae, English stonecrop copes well in long periods of drought. A wildflower of acid soils, this creeping plant clings to rock crevices, steep sides of well-worn footpaths and even sand dunes and shingle above the high tide mark.

Usually a delicate pink but occasionally white, the neat little flowers form dense mats of stars against a background of stubby grey-green leaves that redden in the autumn.

Common Centaury *(Centaurium erythraea)*

15mm

With its uniformly pink (occasionally white) petals this upright biennial is a common and welcome sight on the cliffs and sand dunes of South Wales, where it extends many miles inland. Elsewhere in the Principality it is less common and confined to the coastal strip.

From a basal rosette of oval leaves, on upright stems bearing opposite pairs of leaves clusters of pink, five-petalled flowers appear.

A member of the family Gentianaceae, common centaury thrives in dry, grassy places and is especially common on stable sand dunes and dune slacks.

Centaury is named after the Greek centaur, Chiron, who was half man and half horse. A teacher of the gods, Chiron was skilled in using medicinal herbs. When, accidentally, he was shot by Hercules with a poison arrow, Chiron cured himself using common centaury. Jupiter, believing that Chiron had become too powerful, sent the centaur to heaven, where he is still visible now as the star constellation Sagittarius.

Autumn Gentian *(Gentianella amarella)*

Largely restricted in distribution to nutrient-rich dune slacks along the northern and southern coasts of Wales, where they occur autumn gentians can be found in profusion.

Flowers of the genus *Gentianella* have purple or – as the autumn-flowering example (quite possibly a hybrid) shown on the left – pink flowers. The true gentians, with their deep blue flowers, belong to the genus *Gentiana*, and apart from garden escapes we know of no sites of wild blue gentians on the coast of Wales.

Also included in the gentian family, Gentianaceae, and often found with autumn gentians, are common centaury (facing page) and yellow-wort (see page 59).

Yellow Horned-poppy *(Glaucium flavum)*

A straggly seaside plant with irregular daffodil-yellow flowers, yellow horned-poppy is so called because of its exceptionally long, curved seed pods resembling animal horns.

Yellow horned-poppy grows in shingle above the high-tide mark on many beaches and occasionally on disturbed ground near the sea. In Wales, as indeed elsewhere in the British Isles, this is an increasingly rare species.

The yellow sap that exudes from broken stems of this member of the poppy family, Papaveraceae, is very poisonous.

Bog Pimpernel *(Anagallis tenella)*

> 8mm <

Such a neat little flower, with its shallow lightly-veined pink bells, bog pimpernel thrives in dune slacks and other damp peaty hollows. It is a member of the primrose family, Primulaceae, and like others in the family (such as scarlet pimpernel) opens in sunshine.

Despite its delicate appearance, bog pimpernel is a vigorous perennial and forms dense mats. Each flower is on a separate stem arising from runners that cling stubbornly to the ground.

Jan   Feb   Mar   Apr   May   Jun   Jul   Aug   Sep   Oct   Nov   Dec   *37*

Red Valerian *(Centranthus ruber)*

> 5 <
mm

Branching much more than the **common valerian (*Valeriana officinalis*)** found inland, red valerian is very much a seaside flower, colonising walls, wasteland and shingle banks.

The tiny flowers are usually deep pink, but they can be white. Often, as seen on the left, both colour forms occur together.

Although not a native wildflower, red valerian has become naturalised throughout Wales; it does particularly well in the warmer south of the country and can also be found in some low-lying sites inland.

In locations sheltered from the wind, this attractive perennial member of the valerian family, Valerianaceae, can grow to a metre tall; it provides a wonderful splash of colour in spring, summer and autumn.

Sea Kale *(Crambe maritima)*

Unmistakably a member of the cabbage family, Brassicaceae, sea kale's large curly leaves and dense white flower heads suggest at first glance a gone-to-seed cauliflower. It was from sea kale that many of the cabbage vegetables that we eat today were derived.

Sea kale grows on stable shingle and sand above the high-tide mark.

Once a common seaside plant, sea kale has suffered from the commercialisation of many of the beaches where it once grew in profusion. Fortunately, there are still a few shingle beaches along the coast of North Wales where this distinctive wildflower can be found, including Pensarn Beach, near Abergele, part of which is designated as a Site of Special Scientific Interest (SSSI) for its vegetated shingle and dune grassland, and Cemlyn Lagoon and shingle ridge on Anglesey.

Jan   Feb   Mar   Apr   May   Jun   Jul   Aug   Sep   Oct   Nov   Dec   *39*

Rest-harrow *(Ononis repens)*

The tough stems of this member of the pea family, Fabaceae, are responsible for its common name – a reference to its ability to arrest (stop) the harrow.

Rest-harrow is a wildflower of dry grassland and does best on lime. In southern England it can be found throughout the chalk downland areas as well as on coastal cliffs.

In Wales, rest-harrow is mainly confined to the nutrient-rich strip of land bordering the coast, where it grows on limestone cliffs and, most abundantly, on sand dunes where it helps to stabilise footpaths against erosion by continually trampling feet. Some of the finest summer displays are to be seen beside the coastal footpaths in dune areas.

This is a perennial sprawling plant that spreads rapidly by means of rooting runners.

Vipers Bugloss *(Echium vulgare)*

In a good year some of the coastal cliffs of Wales are covered in swathes of this lovely wildflower. From pink buds the individual funnel-shaped flowers open as brilliant blue racemes up to a metre tall, each flower having four or five purple stamens that protrude well beyond the bell rim.

Both the common and the scientific names of this wildflower have their origins in mythology. Viper's Bugloss was said to be a cure for various poisons, and in particular to counteract the venomous bite of a viper. The white seeds of this plant were also reputed to resemble snakeheads and by this virtue to be a cure for snake bites. The generic name *Echium* is derived from the Latin *echis*, meaning a viper.

These stately wildflowers are not common inland in Wales; they prefer lime-rich grassland.

Very rare in Britain, and currently found only near Land's End, **purple viper's bugloss**, *Echium plantagineum,* (shown left) has flowers very similar to those of viper's bugloss but with a purple tinge and somewhat larger, individual bells being up to 30 mm long. This Mediterranean wildflower of bare places and disturbed land is usually found close to the sea. Although it has not been recorded in Wales in recent times, this short, branched member of the borage family, Boraginaceae, might be expected to extend its range into Wales as global warming changes the climate here.

Southern Marsh-orchid *(Dactylorhiza praetermissa)*

< 40mm >

Most common in South Wales but also found on the West Wales coastal strip, the southern marsh-orchid has dark green leaves that are rarely spotted and flowers usually deep rose-purple but sometimes pink. Dune slacks, marshes and fens are its preferred habitat, but this lime-loving orchid also occurs in damp grassland away from the sea.

Fen Orchid *(Liparis loeselii)*

< 10mm >

The scientific name of this rare orchid is a reference to the seventeenth century Prussian botanist, Johann Loesel. It once grew in more than 30 sites in the UK, but today it can be found in very few places, two of which are in South Wales.

Our picture was taken at Kenfig National Nature Reserve and shows the Welsh subspecies *ovata*, which also flowers on the Burry Inlet. Between them, these two sites contain the majority of the UK's resource of fen orchid plants. Despite its relative abundance in these locations it is remarkably hard to spot, being entirely green and rarely growing to more than 15cm tall.

Although this plant was first found in Wales at Pembrey Burrows, in Carmarthenshire, at the end of the nineteenth century, the fen orchid was not discovered at Kenfig Dunes until 1927.

Jan   Feb   Mar   Apr   May   Jun   Jul   Aug   Sep   Oct   Nov   Dec   *43*

Marsh Helleborine *(Epipactis palustris)*

<   20mm   >

A wild orchid of dune slacks, fens and marshes throughout Wales, the flowers of this lovely helleborine combine in varying proportions crimson, yellow and pure white.

The Marsh helleborine is often acclaimed as our most beautiful wild orchid, perhaps because of its structural similarity to the tropical orchids that are now so popular as house plants and widely available from garden centres and flower shops. Where marsh helleborines occur, the density of plants can be quite spectacular.

Good places for marsh helleborines in Wales include Morfa Dyffryn, between Barmouth and Harlech (part of the Snowdonia National Park), Oxwich Bay on the Gower Peninsula, and the dune systems at Kenfig and at Newborough Warren.

Jan   Feb   Mar   Apr   May   Jun   Jul   Aug   Sep   Oct   Nov   Dec   *45*

Common Twayblade *(Listera ovata)*

'Twa blades' or two blades is the origin of the common name of this very common wild orchid – a reference to the pair of oval leaves at or near the base of the single flower spike.

In ancient times common twayblade flowers were used in ointments to heal wounds.

Lesser twayblade (*Listera cordata*), a miniature version of common twayblade, is much rarer. With an overall reddish tinge and two heart-shaped leaves, this northern species grows to typically 7cm in height. It can be found on the Elan Estate in Powys, on an upland reserve near Lake Vyrnwy, Llanfyllin, and in low montane habitat at Tir Stent, near Dolgellau (a high rainfall area of unimproved rocky grazing land on acidic soil at an altitude below 500 metres).

On sand dune systems all around the coast of Wales common twayblade can be found; it is most abundant on the drier edges of dune slacks and on sheep-grazed coastal cliffs.

Common twayblade, a more adaptable plant than the lesser twayblade, thrives on acidic and calcareous soils, including damp coastal woodland glades.

Although common twayblade can grow to more than 60cm tall, on the windswept coasts where these plants most commonly occur in Wales it is unusual to find specimens more than about half that height. A close-up picture of the flowers of this orchid is shown on the left.

< 10mm >

Tree Lupin *(Lupinus arboreus)*

Not in fact a tree but an evergreen shrub, tree lupin, a native of California, has become widely naturalised on shingle banks and waste ground around the coast of Wales. More common in the south of the country, tree lupin shows a preference for south facing slopes.

< 15mm >

In sheltered locations tree lupins can grow to a height of two metres, but on windswept shores half that height is more the norm. The flowers are usually yellow with a tinge of purple or blue, but occasionally you may find examples that are almost entirely white.

Tree lupin was first brought to the UK in 1793. Because it is so vigorous and spreads easily, this perennial member of the pea family, Fabaceae, has colonised many wasteland sites in Wales. Increasingly this colourful shrub is used for roadside planting, although in exposed locations it can be susceptible to frosts. The flowers have rather a pleasant scent.

Portland Spurge *(Euphorbia portlandica)*

The red-tinged, slightly pointed leaves of this maritime member of the spurge family, Euphorbiaceae, distinguish it from the more common **sea spurge, *Euphorbia paralias*** (below). Both species can be found on cliffs and sand dunes in the south of Wales.

< 20mm >

The strange cup-like flower heads have neither petals nor sepals but merely yellow-green bracts containing the three-pronged (female) styles and a solitary (male) stamen.

In the past, poachers used the poisonous milky sap extracted from stems of various spurges to kill fish.

Common Sea-lavender *(Limonium vulgare)*

> 6mm <

A member of the thrift family, Plumbaginaceae, common sea-lavender grows in great masses on saltmarshes. Unrelated to true lavender save for a similarity of colour, three species of sea-lavender and several subspecies occur in Wales.

In his *Historie of Plants*, published in 1597, the great Elizabethan helbalist John Gerard said of sea-lavender that *'The seed beaten into pouder and drunk with Wine, helpeth the Collique.'*

Jan   Feb   Mar   Apr   May   Jun   Jul   Aug   Sep   Oct   Nov   Dec   *49*

Hottentot-fig *(Carpobrotus edulis)*

75mm

A very common sight in southern Europe and the Mediterranean, this startlingly bright daisy-like flower can also be found in sheltered coastal parts of south Pembrokeshire.

Hottentot-fig forms extensive mats on coastal cliffs, covering near-vertical rock faces with a wonderful display of colour through the summer and autumn months. The petals of this member of the Mesembryanthemun family (Aizoaceae) can be yellow, orange or purple, while the centres are generally pale yellow.

The specific name *'edulis'* suggests that at least some parts of this plant must be edible, and that is indeed true. The tapering waxy leaves, which are triangular in section, certainly are edible, as also are the fig-like brown fruits from which preserves can be made. The Khoihoi (meaning 'men of men') of Namibia, who were also known as the Hottentots, appreciated the water-storing features of this succulent plant.

Sea Holly *(Eryngium maritimum)*

Despite its thistle-like appearance sea holly is an umbellifer. Reputedly a cure for flatulence and indigestion, too much of the cure is more likely to make matters a lot worse.

30mm

In times when this now quite rare wildflower of the carrot family, Apiaceae, was more plentiful, the roots were used as vegetables or for sweetmeats, while the young shoots and leaves served as an asparagus substitute.

Plant collectors who gathered sea holly for food or to create dried flower displays have undoubtedly hastened the decline of this beautiful seaside wildflower.

Jan   Feb   Mar   Apr   May   Jun   Jul   Aug   Sep   Oct   Nov   Dec   *51*

Sea Aster *(Aster tripolium)*

This salt-tolerant plant colonises areas frequently flooded by tides. Where it occurs - on mud flats, estuaries and saltmarshes, for example – sea aster often grows in abundance.

< 16mm >

In Wales, this member of the daisy family, Asteraceae, is found in Pembrokeshire and the South Wales coast as well as in saltmarshes in North Wales. Growing to a typical height of 50cm, the flowers, which resemble Michaelmas daisies, have petals that are usually pale blue-purple but occasionally almost pure white.

In recent years windblown seeds of sea aster have colonised the margins of some main roads that are treated in the winter with salt (and which therefore mimic their preferred saltmarsh habitat).

Bloody Cranesbill *(Geranium sanguineum)*

An uncommon but very welcome sight, the red-purple flowers of bloody cranesbill provide the most wonderful summer displays. In Wales this flower is restricted to a few limestone-rich coastal areas such as South Pembrokeshire and northern Gwynedd.

< 20mm >

The Burren, in Ireland, is famous for its limestone pavement outcrops that are ablaze through the summer months with flowers of bloody cranesbill. Wales has limestone pavement areas too - notably In Denbighshire, on the Great Orme near Llandudno, on parts of the South Pembrokeshire coast, in the Brecon Beacons, and in the Vale of Glamorgan. These are all great places for wildflowers.

There are many colour variations of this member of the family Geraniaceae, but none has petals more blood red than the sepals that remain after the petals have fallen.

Autumn Lady's Tresses *(Spiranthes spiralis)*

Uniquely among the wild orchids of Wales, the creamy-white flowers of this tiny plant – rarely more than 15 to 20cm tall and often no more than 10cm - are arranged in a neat spiral up the stem. Like miniature spiral foxgloves, the lower flowers open first and are often fading before the uppermost flowers open. Backed by small bracts, the green-centred flowers do not have spurs; they are pleasantly scented.

Autumn lady's tresses can be found in dry grassland around the South Wales coast and for quite some distance inland. In Mid Wales this orchid occurs at Ynyslas National Nature Reserve, where staff of the Countryside Council for Wales man the visitor centre from May to September. In South Wales, the finest displays of this fascinating little orchid are usually on flat-topped coastal cliffs such as those at Sker Point, near Kenfig.

With autumn lady's tresses we seem to go through years of plenty and years of famine. The flowers are often recorded as appearing in huge numbers on garden lawns as far apart as Kent and the Gower Peninsula. In some instances many hundreds of spikes will appear in an area of just a few hundred square metres. But then in other years the flowers virtually disappear. There is no doubt that the plants survive under the ground, their numbers seemingly unaffected by these non-flowering periods, because a year or so later they are back in numbers as great as ever.

Despite its relative abundance most years, this intriguing wildflower can really take some finding. Because the basal leaves wither before the flowers appear, it can be very difficult indeed to spot theses tiny orchids in anything but the shortest of sheep-grazed turf.

Wild Thyme *(Thymus polytrichus)*

On dunes and coastal cliffs wild thyme creates dense mats topped with whorls of pink-purple flowers. This lime-loving wildflower also occurs in mountainous areas.

> 6mm <

This aromatic plant from the family Lamiaceae attracts a variety of insects. In the picture on the left a burnet moth is collecting nectar from the flowers of wild thyme.

Wild thyme can be used in cooking, and in common with other species of thyme it also contains the chemical thymol, which is a strong antiseptic.

In the past, posies containing wild thyme were used to ward off infectious diseases, and sprigs were placed under the pillow at night to promote sleep. Thyme has also been used to make a kind of tea and to scent clothes and household linens.

Dewberry *(Rubus caesius)*

< 20mm >

A low-growing relative of the familiar bramble, or blackberry, the true dewberry has white flowers, but its hybrids with other bramble species often have pinkish flowers.

Common on coastal cliffs and in particular on sand dunes in Wales, dewberries, which belong to the rose family, Rosaceae, also occur occasionally on woodland edges and in scrubby field margins.

Throughout the summer and autumn months the blue-black fruits can be gathered for jam making. The waxy bloom on these fruits and their generally fewer but larger segments compared with brambles are distinguishing features. The berries are sweet and not quite as strong in flavour as brambles.

Burnet Rose *(Rosa pimpinellifolia)*

Common along the west coast of Wales but most abundant on dune systems in South Wales, this lovely member of the rose family, Rosaceae, rarely grows taller than 30cm.

< 30mm >

The burnet rose is a lime-loving species generally associated with chalk downland or limestone pavement habitats. It has five cream or pink-tinged flowers in summer and purple-black hips that persist through the winter months.

Yellow-wort *(Blackstonia perfoliata)*

Grey-green leaves, joined in pairs to form cups up the stem, and bright yellow flowers make yellow-wort stand out even among such splendid wildflowers as the autumn gentians and marsh helleborines, with which they tend to occur.

In Wales, the dunes along the northern and southern coastal strips – and particularly the marshy dune slacks – are where this lime-loving wildflower can be seen in greatest numbers.

While the flowers of other members of the family Gentianaceae have either four or five petals, yellow-wort is distinguished by having at least six and usually eight flower petals.

Only in the brightest sunshine do the flowers of yellow-wort open fully, and even on the warmest of summer days they close very quickly whenever a cloud passes across the sun.

The Latin name of this plant is a reference to the 18th Century botanist and apothecary John Blackstone.

18mm

Common Milkwort *(Polygala vulgaris)*

Common milkwort and its smaller relative **heath milkwort (*Polygala serpyllifolia*)** are found throughout Wales, but they are at their showiest on the short turf of coastal cliifs.

< 6mm >

Although common milkwort can grow to a height of 30cm, half this height is more usual. Heath milkwort is a slightly smaller plant with smaller and usually paler flowers; its lower leaves are paired (opposite) whereas those of common milkwort are always alternate.

Milkworts are all members of the family Polygalaceae; their flowers can be blue, pink, mauve or occasionally white.

Common milkwort tends to favour lime-rich soils, while heath milkwort occurs more often on acid grassland.

Jan   Feb   Mar   Apr   May   Jun   Jul   Aug   Sep   Oct   Nov   Dec

Sea Rocket *(Cakile maritima)*

Varying in colour from very pale lilac to pink or sometimes violet, the four-petalled flowers of sea rocket help to identify it as a member of the cabbage family, Brassicaceae.

< 15mm >

Usually found on the strand line - where driftwood and other flotsam collect after spring (the highest) tides – sea rocket grows on sand or occasionally on sandy shingle.

The sand dart moth feeds on sea rocket (and also on sea-holly - see page 51).

Chicory *(Cichorium intybus)*

35mm

This heavenly blue flower is Wales's only native blue dandelion-like wildflower.

On spindly plants growing up to a metre tall, the unstalked flowers are scattered randomly along the stems.

Although Chicory, a member of the family Asteraceae, can appear on roadsides and waste ground almost anywhere, in Wales it is mainly confined to locations close to the sea where the soil is predominantly lime-based.

Chicory has been cultivated as a herb since the sixteenth century. Young shoots of chicory can be used in salads: white spears of leaves are produced by forcing them to grow in darkness or under flower-pots. The dried and ground roots have been used as a substitute for (or as an additive to) coffee.

Bugloss *(Anchusa arvensis)*

A close relative of **green alkanet (*Pentaglottis sempervirens*)** which is most commonly found in hedgerows, in Wales bugloss is mainly a coastal and estuarine wildflower. It has very rough, wavy and slightly prickly leaves.

< 6mm >

Bugloss is shorter and its flowers, once they are fully open, are rather bluer than those of its more conspicuous relative **vipers bugloss (*Echium vulgare*)** which is sometimes closer to purple.

In common with alkanets, comfreys, forget-me-nots, gromwells and lungworts, the various bugloss species are members of the borage family, Boraginaceae.

Jan   Feb   Mar   Apr   May   Jun   Jul   Aug   Sep   Oct   Nov   Dec   *63*

Common Broomrape *(Orobanche minor)*

These fascinating leafless plants closely resemble some of our wild orchid species. Containing no chlorophyll, the source of green pigment in plants, broomrapes cannot make direct use of the sun's energy. They are parasitic and depend on other host plants for their source of food.

Broomrapes, of which at least four species occur in Wales, are difficult to identify with certainty. Often the proximity of the host plant is the only way to be sure which broomrape you have found.

The specimen pictured here is common broomrape, which can grow to more than half a metre (30cm is more typical) and has numerous hosts including clover and wild carrot. The flowers are usually reddish-brown with violet veins.

In sheltered locations dead flower heads of common broomrape often remain standing well into the winter months.

The picture on the left was taken at the base of the first line of stable sand dunes at Kenfig National Nature Reserve. Here, common broomrape appears to be parasitising sea holly (see page 51). Such an assumption might be precipitous, however: there were various members of the pea family (Fabaceae) growing within two or three metres, and it might well be their roots upon which these broomrapes were feeding.

Broomrapes, members of the family Orobanchaceae, are lime-loving plants and so they are rarely seen in the wild in Wales very far from the sea.

Occasionally broomrapes will appear in gardens, where they parasitise plants that are closely related to the hosts that they attack in the wild.

Sticky Storksbill *(Erodium lebelii)*

< 20mm >

This short, straggly annual wildflower colonises the edges of well-trodden footpaths in dune systems near the sea in South Wales. The storksbills are notoriously difficult to identify to species level with certainty; with this species the sticky hairs, often sand-coated, are a help.

Being a low-growing plant among many more plentiful and taller wildflowers, sticky storksbill often escapes attention.

Storksbills generally have smaller flowers than their close relatives the cranesbills – the latter distinguished also by their deeply cut palmate leaves. (Both groups are members of the family Geraniaceae). Once storksbill flower petals have fallen, the seeds develop in beaked pods that are spirally twisted (inset, above).

Several alien storksbill species occur in Wales; they are mainly restricted to improved grassland.

Jan   Feb   Mar   Apr   May   Jun   Jul   Aug   Sep   Oct   Nov   Dec

Caring for Coastal Wildflower Habitats

The Countryside Council for Wales (www.ccw.gov.uk) is our national conservation authority and advisor to Government, Local Authorities and others on sustaining the natural beauty and wildlife of Wales and on increasing the opportunities for enjoyment of the countryside.

CCW cannot do much of this alone. The physical diversity of our coastline makes it attractive for numerous forms of enterprise and recreation, and so it is hardly surprising that many organisations have responsibility for managing those uses and, by implication at least, an obligation to contribute to protecting the coastal environment. CCW therefore works in partnership with many other governmental agencies, trusts and voluntary bodies.

The National Trust (www.nationaltrust.org.uk) owns nearly 150 miles of coastline in Wales, while some of the RSPB's finest bird reserves in Wales (www.rspb.org.uk/wales) are on river estuaries – for example at Ynyshir, on the tidal Dyfi near Machynlleth, and at Penmaenpool, on the Mawddach Estuary near Dolgellau.

Pembrokeshire and Snowdonia National Parks (www.cnp.org.uk) also border the sea on their westward side, while the Forestry Commission (www.forestry.gov.uk/wales) is a partner in the management of part of the Newborough Warren Nature Reserve. The Woodland Trust also looks after many woodland sites in Wales that overlook the sea.

The Wildlife Trust movement (www.wildlifetrust.org) manages conservation sites and reserves throughout Wales. For example, Cardigan Wildlife Park, on the Teifi Estuary in West Wales, and Morfa Bychan, near Porthmadoc in North Wales provide some wonderful habitats for coastal wildflowers.

In Wales the unitary authorities are also actively involved in the management of reserves and in publicising the opportunities that these ecological oases provide for the study and enjoyment of Nature. For example Bridgend County Council supports a wonderful National Nature Reserve at Kenfig Dunes. A bonus of visiting such designated sites and reserves is the chance to meet the rangers, wardens and conservation volunteers, who share so generously their wealth of knowledge. We have always been inspired by their infectious passion for the Welsh countryside that they care for.